Shelter The Messenger

Selected Poetry of Gregory M George

Shelter The Messenger

Copyright © 2010 Mitchell George

All rights reserved.

ISBN: 1466398965

Shelter The Messenger

"The newly re-invented Charles Bukowski has been born!"

   -Blog Subscriber

"Somewhere in the middle is Mitchell George with a book of life, half crazy as hell and half beautiful poetry. Finally is this the word wizard extraordinaire we've been looking for?"

   -Cody Wood

"Wow Mitch, that's incredibly inspiring, that could be something that could even change hundreds of people's lives. It's amazing. Great things can come from those you least expect.."

   -Homeschool (undisclosed user)

"The way you can bring things to its true value makes me more envious than anything else could.
That was amazing."

   -*R3TRO* (undisclosed user)

Gregory M George

Dedication

>Those who walked me home

Acknowledgments

I would like to thank...

Everyone that decided to stick around at my worst times and stay with me to experience the good times, although there were rough patches between the two, you are all much appreciated.

I would also like to thank my subscribers and everyone who gave me that final push to continue writing no matter how much I was going through at the time. Your inspiration and support has allowed me to finally release some of the poetry I never thought I would ever publically show. The poetry that has branded my web blogs and social networking notes, along with my journals has been cut and selected specifically for all of you, my greatest support.

Shelter The Messenger

Contents

I am a very un-organized person,
so is my book.

Gregory M George

Introduction

Twenty years old and I'm sitting in front of my computer screen reminiscing about my eventful past; this is what I choose to do instead of getting shit faced in the country or doing new street drugs with the boys while drooling like poorly drawn coyotes over some tail.

Most people would wonder why someone would choose writing over the extreme extravaganza of adolescent drugs and alcohol use. Well you see. Most twenty year olds have structured lives with safe childhoods and a good grasp of wealth or proper parenting. Most children are forced to go to school while being homed and fed under a rent free home. I unfortunately was never lucky enough to have such a lifestyle.

I have chosen writing as my therapy, my personal choice to overcome life's adversities. Anything that was bothering me I wrote it down, my life is a pencil and paper. With the publishing of this book, I kept everything the way it was, spelling mistakes and all. The main reason I decided to do the Shelter The Messenger project was because I wanted to show the world what writing can do for a person. How powerful it can be to a person just to release whatever is on their mind without any worry at all. When the moods are taking advantage of you take advantage of them and turn them into art.

I want readers to know that these poems were written from drugs, alcohol and emotional abuse, this is what came out of my mind in a very dark time of my life, and this is what helped me get through such low and unfortunate events. I was once black and white, I now see color in all angles of my life, I am now happy. I have very little satisfaction in entertaining such dark thoughts anymore.

I know there are many ways to relief yourself of mental slavery, be it with music or writing, or anything that lets you let your mind move to the rhythm of a freedom breeze, but I promise to you writing is a very helpful resource. It has become my main therapeutic release.

I know some of the things inside of this book will be very confusing as if there is a door you must unlock in order to understand it. I re assure you there is no alternative language or speaking in tongues going on here, strictly metaphors.

I will inform you once again this wasn't just written from one moment to the next, these poems of literature have been in the process of being built in to the "Shelter The Messenger Project" for a few years now. Guaranteed this is absolutely not your typical average book. The collection of poetry is created from inheriting most of my darkest and deepest journal entries and thoughts. Presented with the effects of drug use, alcoholism and the threatening lifestyle of a known stain this will leave most of you confused and curious. With meaningless rants, dark poetry, and nothing but my honest heart, you will find yourselves reading the new age poetry that entertains our dark and deepest satisfaction in artistic release.

This is what I wrote down in the last few years, this was me.

Shelter The Messenger

<u>Were all dumb</u>

I still blame my father for all the fucking wasted time and years in my life, he has been forgiven

Shelter The Messenger

<u>Indeed</u>

The legs of a woman are such a beautiful feature,

Spider man is such old news

Shelter The Messenger

<u>Jill</u>

It's weird how one person, just one person could
change the way you feel, the way you feel about
yourself and your surroundings, but someone you never
knew too well, but with just a smile, could make
your dreams achieved. A wonderful person, who could make you feel
accepted.

Shelter The Messenger

<u>Goodbye Brother</u>

I will stand here, I feel like I'm fine today.

Life's and adventure, things happen, things come, and things go.

Tell me, what do you do or say to such a sudden remark. Me, I did what I usually do, I just ignored it. What a dumb fucking idea. Taking the pain is life. Numbing the pain is avoiding your problems in life. A flower, a best friend, is like a deer and her youngling. Time comes where the road splits. And following that road is life. Remember. No looking back.

Ladies & gentlemen, I have reached the fork.

Like said
may the birds walk,
The fish fly.
Humans love,
and cowards lie.

I Will Be Waiting.

Gregory M George

Maniac People on Our Streets

Hey girl, I've got a place to relax,
Hey girl, I'm your best friend remember that.

Do you remember the day we met?
Do you remember the day of your death?
The time you set sail, oceans boat,
casted away, after slitting your throat.
When the blood soaked through,
do you remember what I said to you..
I do...

Shave Your Pencils

Touch my fantasy..

She sits on trees, picking cherries alone.
The beast who craved the hood, now seeks the throne.
One dead baby who holds the crown
at last will be found,
digging up her bones.
The candle eats the bloody shoes, masks of violence that leave,

NO FUCKING CLUES

just ask Alice when she's ten feet tall.

Gregory M George

Are You That Desperate For My Heart?

To those birds that walk,
and fish who fly,
the penny on the street
alone and worthless,
left abandoned by feet.

Letting me let the wrong ones in,
leaving the sun to make me remember,
those who sin
are not cowards.

It's cruel how this world,
is filled with those who rape
innocent little girls.

Stand next to me,
not behind me.
Stand next to me,
not in front of me.
Stand next to me,
not within me.

I met a blind man
who taught me how to read the bible,
who lit a candle
for there was not enough moonlight?

Set me free,

Let the worthless, stand next to me.

Greed Insects

I called the vampires from the farthest distant,
they were naked and covered in blood.
They let me walk inside and cover my face,
I woke up in the light.

Dogs were drinking from mugs, and paper bags had breathing lungs.
I watched the liquor drink itself,
and the trees were prisoned by abuse.
The wind blows and I refuse,
I shouldn't let go.

We stare at ourselves from a distant,
but nobody understands what they see.
because we believe were only ourselves when we achieve,
mistakes are withdrawn from the lives we lead.

Nobody believes who they are,
not even me.

Next Step

Draw this you punk,

Bucket of water,
rope.
Letter to the dogs,
recipe.

I want your muddy broom,
to clean up this mess,
don't blame me, I create.
Jump.

Recipe,
for all the reasons you need,
to feel comfort.
Don't step backwards,
give up,
give in,

Listen.

Apology

You,

and me, were nothing but the worlds beauty,
with struggle and disease,
we were everything that people couldn't stand to believe.
Living as if we were free of worry.

I still feel you, as if we were swimming into the car crash.
The crash that killed you and everything I ever believed,
the incident that took away a part of me, everything I ever believed.
I am not a part of your life, you're in the sky, I'm here waiting to die.
I hate it, I want to die, no fear in saying it.

It's just, oh my apology.
my. oh my fault, I apologize for not being that someone,
picking up my feet to find new meaning, we scream.
Breaking glass and fumes, Just remember,
I always loved, loving you.

I get by knowing the futures nothing but dull moments,
sold out performers and abortions on the clinics bill,
health care, everyone's going to hell.
I said it, heavens not real.
I'm scared nobody's going to be home.
swimming,

Gregory M George

I'm Wrong

I want your vaginal Discharge on my face..
That bubble between your teeth when you talk.

The conscious thoughts of rape...
Figure out what's wrong..
Blame myself for being..

Too much like someone else.

You Can't Get Me

Puke From Pain, ask any man.
Eat your own blood, and cause a night.
Then you'll understand.

Cement Bars

We grow between the thoughts
that never make appearances,
we eat at the table of Christ,
and bathe with the water we pee in.

Make me an honest man,
beyond the hair that grows on your face
this is just like when we use to dance with our feet,
when we were human, the days we were allowed to breathe.
Alone, alone, were making decisions..

We cannot regret, oh yeah, yeah.
I'm so high, high, yeah.
I promise I will be okay, I promise I will always worship,
I mend it and pray, I cannot do it today.
Yeahhhh.... I'd rather laugh, I want to play.
I can't do this today.

Diet With Powdered Fantasy

I'm demented and a liar. Egghead

Gregory M George

<u>You Just Can't Kill</u>

Let me be in 1969.

And let me check in.
and grab a drink.

My surprise,

I'll promise to never leave.
Ill be your prisoner.

Bomb This Letter

Just turn the radio down,
and listen, I'm a fool,

I'll eat the splinter, if you pull it out.
I'll live in the jar, if you put it away.

Mornings here,

I'll leave, if you give me back my head.

Heroine

The heroine absorbed, I had to take a shit..
I'll never shit on heroine again, ever.
This whole thing is something I'm not use too.

I'm on my own,

filling my head with these things,
pistol aims,
I escaped.
The gates with my life.

Hair Fall

If girls smoke their hair will smell bad.

She Hit Me

I created this friend,
not obtained.
Created.

I'm a freak, but I love nature.
I'm gay, but I love this girl.
I'm dumb, but yet I'm happy.
I'm warm, but so violent.

Welcome to Imagination.

Casino Toilets Don't Flush

I woke up to you..

I talked and didn't give in, you're the despise,
you wanted to see me.

But you also lied and said you wouldn't give up so easy

I think it's through....
remember it takes two.

Jacks got your queen.

Wheat and Farmers Thoughts

I throw myself towards the lies.

Goodbye misery,
goodbye those awful thoughts.

What's that? Is he yours?
No, no, I lie too much.

Let me be your queen and sleep in the rain,
I'll walk away just to let you,
absorb the wonders of this.

I didn't know you this whole time along?
Was it me or you, who was wrong?

Echo..

Preach it, eat it, Cunt.

Live and let live,

Agony, is mine.

Give Me Back My Alcohol

I don't like that shadow..
I hold it in my hands..
Do not come alive..

I Beg for.

Sue to be on the other side

Gregory M George

<u>You're The Only Way to Shop</u>

I don't care that you make me voiceless..

I'M NOT FUCKING ALONE,
I will never be alone.

It's what you had to say just to eat that plate;
I will sit here and wait for the rain.
Come to wash away my face.

These are the things I hate,
here, right now.

Horses Come and Horses Go

I continue to ask myself, where is home?
I lie every single night,
when I close my eyes I tear from my seams.

Oh god, I cannot believe,
this is what I have become tonight.
I scream for someone to turn the light on,
I dream of almost finding you,
since the moment you left,
why haven't you stayed,
why on earth do you always run away,
why, why can't I touch you tonight,
just one last time.

Is it because you died?
That means nothing, your still here,
in me, I feel you come alive,
all the time.

Why the fuck wont you come,
why the fuck wont you answer me,
why the fuck did you leave.
Where is my mom,

It's obvious to say,
it's you I've become.

It's Yours

Don't deny, the fuck that.
I don't type this shit.

My mind does.
I control my liquor not my words...

Read it and eat it people.
Don't deny it.
I'm an ugly person...

I hope you enjoy my life.
It's like the sun, it's for you.

All Fired Up

I know you cannot lie to me,

I know you still love me, just the way you did.

seeing the pretending the puppets did,

the way they moved on stage.

It caught my eye, did you notice?

It stings my eyes, it stings my eyes, I cannot find my hat.

If you see me burning down, committing suicide,

do not breakdown on my side.

There's nothing here for you to climb,

it's a lovely pot of gold,

and it's not your matter!

It's the biggest piece of shit in the world,

and nobody can justify the drugs I'm on,

im the tallest man in the world right now.

Gregory M George

That fucking asshole just had to get me all fired up,

he got me all fired up, all fired up.

I wanna get more fired up.

Time Your Bombs Love

I think my father just killed our dog.
Time to grow up and give sympathy,
Why do I lie?
Why the fuck is she with me?

I'm sleeping with your daughter, I'm the prick.
I'm the one tasting her cum filled lipstick.

She's got both hands on my junk, we spit blood.

Rape me father, rape me.

Mother Sings

Hey, Cinderella, I'm holding you in my dreams,
underneath the apple tree.

Spank through the sun,
my head hurts, and so do my eyes.
I hate what I see,
this despise.

I can fix you, if you can fix me.

She Hides Her Words Somewhere

I feel your body sweat and pussy juice on my open wounds,
I feel a break in the neck of the innocent.
I'm bigger.

I don't quit till I see light,
then I do with no regrets, sleep fine at night.

Can I draw you mutilated?
Can you for fill my fantasy.
Let me fuck it, again, and again.
Just fuck it.
Till you whimper and bleed.

Bloodshot is to cold.
Air is too hot.
Pain is perfect.

Keep it coming.

Territory Trace

Yes I can hear you,
I can hear the screaming,
Its better then mine,
dont explain,
I wont divide,
I want to be a transvestite,
I want to be a whole,
but nothing makes it work,
I have a penis, and you know,
my piss stained matress we cant throw out,
it has memory,
and smell,

Thats one story you cannot re-tell,
this is ours, I will always,
I will sacrifice my life,
to sleep on this mattress one more time,
to sleep in what was once mine,

It's always mine, i just want to make sure,
the other persons is dirt poor,
and sleeps comfortably shy,
on the bed, I PISSED,
the bed I marked I.

One for Me One for You

She is making me feel so reassured,
but it feels like,
this forest fire is burning me alive.

It's like a maze, where all the walls continuously change.

Favourite D

I have found you, in almost all the places I have been.

I beg for you, to get out of my head,

I see you in the lillies,

It seems like just yesterday I watched you runaway,

I see you in the wind, that blows into tomorrow,

I dont want to think about you as forever ago.

Ive accepted to live without you, then live without truth,

I follow these morals of mine,

just to look the other way,

and wait, to get fucked over another time,

your always on my damn mind.

Across My Chest

There's this boy I know, the way he plays his piano almost as
distinctive as the way he speaks. With his eyes closed I feel
the need to be attracted to the spit that holds his top lip to his
jittering bottom lip,
living with his darling, who loves me too.

I want the world to see that we met; I want the world to know.
I dream of his girl all night, the disguised acidic bubbles she
blows, there's nothing we can do, but learn to be here in sound.

All they need is love.

Would you hold my hand, if I told you, I loved you.

Together our sweaty palms will hold us, and let the birds
guide the way, the sunken yellow birds sing.

While, we learn to fly,

Yeah,
What would they do, if I sang them a song,
About being alone.
Walking through the wrong fields,

I'm on my own.
I want them to see what I see, when I look at this light.
I don't need anybody,
just somebody to love.

Gregory M George

Secret Worlds with Alternate Endings

Will things be the same,
after all these mind games?

What am I going to do with myself?

Rockstar Forget

Up and beat, she sounded so sweet
I spoke, god, I was nervous, I couldn't speak.
I was alone, when I saw her, I said no.
She walked past me, I was drunk,

god letting her go,
made me feel so alone,

that night I took a shit,
after her I named it,
Crowd cheered on we went,
flush, down she went.

Gregory M George

Five o Clock

Sadly, I can't sleep tonight.

The white noise from that TV
is surprisingly out of reach.

I Smoke Cigarettes

I don't even want to count the days,
I miss her soo much.
I can't even explain.

S Company

Addicted to the puppet,
No more recess, I don't need to smoke, or feel the rising heat.
As long as the cherry, burns in front of me.

I just need to drown out, close my eyes, never blink.
Need time to fade,
time to think.

Let me free;
let the liquor take care of me.

<u>7 am</u>

I'm tearing my heart out and putting it on this chain, which is
disgustingly covered in flesh that barely holds its base,
in an arousing manner, it was like a warm fish on a Sunday's
fishhook.

I have been putting myself there,
I fish alone.
As I lay on the grass,
as we say, yeahhhhh.

Dew

Play it hard,
play it quick,
don't say it, I dont need your forgivness.

Die Mother Fucker.

Tell me, what gives you the pain?
Who gives you approval?

Just go home,
respect the ways
of being alone,

bring the dead home.

Dreaming of Letting My Hands Down

When it's through, it's through.

Don't get me wrong, adolescents will never change.
Rape your prom date, waste another day.
SOMEBODY GET ME OUT OF HERE!
Is this the world that's worth dying for? Are you ready to
never stand up, never taste blood? Or never eat cement?
Always do what you're told and live the way they preach.

Create a midnight soundtrack and get out there, but never aim for the
imperfection, keep your head up, always blow someone off.

Whats wrong with being happy? Trust me, it feels good when
you feel it, so happy.

I look down and blink for a moment of a second,
I see destruction, I love it.

The destruction of yourself,
the dwelling hands hovering over "Self Destruct".
Sounds so appealing, but who's ready to die for this world?
For it, we call defeat.

I'll go for the lead role, you can wear my smile.
Its only limited, yeah, alone, alone, alone.
I'll pick a flower for you and give it to them, kill a living
plant, because I just gave in.
Come on, It's in my hands. Come closer.

Star

Oh, mirror in the sky, what is love?

Hey George

What If Curious George went back to the jungle,
would things still be the same?
Would he miss the man in the yellow hat?

I Don't Remember Losing Hope

I'm not scared...

I just threw away my radio,
my spiders ate my piano.
I threw away my telephone;
I think I know my friends, watching them scream.

Another argument and bitter love,
I hate being alone,
anger.
Punching windows made of cement,

Im so faceless,
but so innocent...

Am I this contagious?

We are the waiting.

Chips and Drinks

You know, I still find you dashing.

Gregory M George

<u>Fun House Tears</u>

You may kiss the bride,
the new, "Mr. Murder"

Discarding shoes,
and killing highways.

Reality

Guys are lame,
and girls are annoying.

Nobody will take my mother's place.

Snoring Stinky Imagination

Some sort of window that kills the pain, through the glass we see,
reality starts to cry, we feel rain,
in an instance, we are always wrong, I pray to someone's god
that you will survive, I will look after you, I will stay alive.

and who chooses where we should be right now,
I know where I am, and where I have been,

unsure and insecure, timid, were all born pure.
ring on my finger, we find religion our passion,
corrupted, stinky, fashion.

Jesus dies one brave Jew,
un safe from the superior at our own cost,

I would of joined in, I would of hung him on the cross.

True Reality

It's exactly like the quote from the books I'm reading;

you will love the mask, but will you love what's behind it?
The mask has many stories to please your soul, but whoever reveals hidden has only stories to torture you whole.

I fell for this, my whole life, Im always the fucking underdog.
Clue-less old me to leave someone with no voice,

I only ask one question...

May I try on the mask?

Gregory M George

<u>True Reality Take 2</u>

Beneath this mask

I am just a loser.

Sports Car

Curled up, I scream,

leather interior is faded with fabric,

the mirror is jaded with non existence,

I live inside of misery,

in the womb of this car,

I will be re-born.

I will be your hero,

Suicide is not an option,

Wrong or right,

I will be a god in my next life,

I cant stop thinking about birth and death tonight.

Belly

Told myself I wouldn't do this, it always ends the same.

It's always constant, I lead myself to shame.

Ah, I hate being soo...I dont know any good words to explain.

I'm just so embarrassed, and so disappointed in myself.

Day

I'm overjoyed, but senseless,

over protective and very insecure.

I want it all, but there were no takers.

I am the Insecurity Guard.

Gregory M George

Viva la, lose it all

This stupid fucking dog blanket
smells like shit, I want to sleep,
I want my own fucking bed,
I want one so bad.
I want a genie,
to wish me shelter,
clothing,
and food.
I want it,
I want a
drugdealer too,
he wont
get through,
me,
I think im
pretty fucking
doomed.

Separate...

Your Voice Is A Gift

I ask myself, am I fighting this war,
just to leave home wounded and empty handed?

No,

Those who fight, fight for pride and love.
Only those who fight for these reasons,
are ready to take defeat.

Gregory M George

The Unspeakable

I guess I don't write much anymore because there's nothing to write.

Everything has just turned into, nonsense.

Take what you have, and open all your doors.

Stop creating paths or even following them,

I will write again,

when I get over this wall of obscure,

words,

and worlds.

Are You Ready?

Hey you, go fuck yourself!

Crashing planes and dead cashiers,

Innocents of non-believers, these do not occur in my occasion,

for the fact of the devil,

we bring revelation.

Gregory M George

Always About You

If you didn't scream so loud,

I would kill you,

Shedding blood, you know taste me?

If you danced with the tortured,

Id be happy

That's The Life

Porn mags, ash trays and video games.

Laugh It Layla

La la la la la la la!

How does it feel to go against your morals?

I Am Naked and Fearless

Hatred keeps me alive,

ugliness keeps me alive,

weakness keeps me alive,

guilt keeps me alive,

at the bottom.

I SHOT HIM DEAD.

Tulip Flavor

Dancing was the light inside your dreams,
the rivers were calm and she insisted on following me,
love isn't real anymore.
Love was created by the man with horns,
we called his bluff when he created the rose with thorns.

We never knew, we never know, what's right.
Love cannot be so innocent, it tends to bite.
We never knew, we never know, what's right.
we taste tulip wine, and follow our breath tonight.

Skinless Women

Breath with pregnancy,
grow with flowers
and
spend more time with me.
Tuning voices with farm animals,
they become meat.

Conquer your hate,
drug an underage,
underwater she can swim,
no sin.
she pulls on your foreskin.

Brothers I love, three of us,
regret overwhelms,
 crawling back into fetus.
I am growing weak
mother forgot to turn cheek.

kill for food and not for fur,
religion hunted for her.

In A Sense, She's A Rainbow

Mother!

DISGUISE ME!

Show me, what a world of color really is,

I only see her true colors.

I'd rather black & white.

Bring me home.

Comfort Lies Somewhere

It's a lot easier to believe,

Fiction is my future.

Be you.

Whoever arms you lay in.

Be you.

Gregory M George

Look Back and Talk With Me

He told me to only love those who love you.

I said, I will love those that I love,

and those that I hate.

I can't wait to meet you there.

My will is good.

I Hurt My Brain

Well I guess, we write these writings just to say it.

We can brush it off, whatever; I don't even know what I write.

Maybe I'm lazy.

I'm dangerous.

Make sure you're self-assured, because your opinions are yours,

Even if you make them up or write them between lazy metaphors of obstruction, sometimes we aim for the less, instead of the greats.

I can't wait, to fulfill fantasies of my greats,

and your worst.

No need to apply, I think we all have the artistic license.

No need to learn.

Hello.

Your hair on your fore arms, are extremely entertaining.

Sit on the little ones, no masturbation, just games.

Be an addiction.

Make positive damages.

If you are going to be ready, wear a dress.

A ghost of when it happened.

Are you a qweer or something?

Because my mother is a girl and she can pull hair.

Pull mine.

WAIT!

Hi, how are you?

Don't smoke near my ocean, and dont expect me to write about my misery,

that's my goal.

This Is A Drug

When you tried to make that plant grow, you must have been high. You don't win in till you pull it out, but how long will you reach inside of yourself?

Yeah he's the one, but was never the only one.

Was he love, or was he a friend?

Vomit expels, and projects from all your open sores, not your memory. Your cosmetic water glistens with flowers.

Take advantage, of grandmother's lungs.

 See me every night.

Twitch & masturbate.

You're always laughing when its way to loud, you can cough on me when you're dreaming. This is way too much like them, please don't be dreaming.

You're such a horse with aggression, of a female mind.

For once, call me dumb.

She thinks you consume the artificial, but you consume hearts, some are broke.

If you inhaled the hangover, we would call for your wisdom.

Gregory M George

Does she think she is the sun, or are you the one?

Give you a wake up, lesson her or just pretend.

If you had cancer, I would tell you to wait, so I could survive.

Cut your flesh, how bad did you want it?

Forget what birds say.

Nine to eleven.

What If I told you, to never say a word again? Would you pray for pain? Or envy all your fear? Because I believe in idolism, but I never hide.

One day, you will realize you are right,

listen to the melody.

Won't somebody save this lady from me?

Natural Flavor

I blame myself,

for thinking how safe the smallest string,

could actually be.

My eyes can see,

they seek out all your empty threads.

Yeah, nearly.

This secret,

you should look cute without the five.

That's me, all me.

Are you satisfied?

Gregory M George

<u>Motorboat</u>

Feeling like a story,
it was cold.
furry white snow
she was nothing but odd.
I had myself a
Friend
something I could hold,
she's running
through seasons and playing in the mirror.

Substitutes will be well unknown.

What To Do

Me,

I am the man, the one who sells worlds to those who rob grave yards.

I am not your man,

but the cancer of your lips.

Gregory M George

<u>Here With You & Me</u>

Dont worry, you will find yourself.

It's you, do you understand?

I can do this, let me try.

What do you want, what's in you, the gold?

Let's take an attempt, let's be some kind of simple.

Who are we? The hair on our face, is what we spare,

from the innocence of our lives,

then you say you know what it's like.

What if i said, It would be alright,

would you try to attempt to stay alive.

If there is something wrong, dont grab her.

She is making you feel like you said, alright.

Hey girl, you're my best friend, remember that,

I have a place we can releax,

YOU are my journal,

Shelter The Messenger

you are the worse in me,

SAY it.

Please, say it to me.

You heard it all before, Hold it.

I'm not your future; I am your present,

for as long as you want to feel dry, paint me grey.

Your bright colors, It hurts the eyes.

Don't bleed in your health,

this is my only true view,

where is my bathroom stall, I am way to soft spoken.

Let's be you,

for one day, let me have your views.

Your lips, your glasses they make me dry,

Drive to the hills, and we will go to the point of feel.

Together, were alone and your highly advanced, I want to stay away,

Slap the eyes of her, and the little child.

I'm the juvenile.

I'm the friend.

MERCY, have me be, have me broken.

You're everything you must be,

dont have my rhyme, Its just the noise dowsntairs,

he said it was good, I wanted to wait,

does she love, or wait?

It's only you and me here.

Let's be denied.

I will hope to believe it's a dream,

This means nothing to me,

It's me.

<u>Earn</u>

Feed me what you have left over,

bring me the stations.

My teacher, she smells like Halloween.

Gregory M George

<u>Inspired Sick</u>

Sweet apple, where is your communication?

Music have you taken my generation?

Mother's spirit, and all of my father's hate,

is it all for me?

All of these chains are like waves,

telling me it's time.

That sound, that sound of angels.

It hurts my ears, why? My religion why?

Am I just nothing, nothing to you?

These are not my enforcements or power of equality.

It Begins In The Wrist

Can you smell that? Oh god, that's wonderful!

Sunshine in the bedroom, are you up? Do you play?

Difference with me, is that what you're going to say?

I learned it all, yeah time to move on.

Your way to silent, still it's you and I.

What going on?

I hear the coming of....WHAT COME ON! What's my name?

It's operating the occasion, are you mental framing my physical!!

Media, where is today? Preach truth, show me family.

Scratch, show me what goes on! Don't have the body?

Brother's loyalty!

Nobody like you, nobody wants you, Jesus and his fun.

Are you gone yet?

She said she would, God where is her lips?

Oh god, does any one care? Does anyone think?

This is about my favorite tragedy!

Nobody cares.

You are what you preach. Come.

Never sing rhythm, or hymns for the dead.

Its' not worth your witnessed days,

I could of lied, im no minor.

Roll your tounge and sing.

The world cried the tears you dropped,

can you show your teeth?

Killing myself to photographs,

dolls are perfect, stop wasting your smiles and just escape your skin.

Float your smile; I am your little light, carry the moon.

Popularity fades too soon.

I was homeless, but no bridge.

The legends,

they never receive my kiss.

I am me, me with no partner, shirtless, and sun glasses.

Addiction is my companion.

Shelter The Messenger

Show me what you have,

silver screens, my masturbation.

Baby, I am the world.

Get out, your closet is empty, I read your book and I'm impressed.

No birds, no birds. I fell over my taste for you.

It took two people to push, writings on the toilets in this stall.

I can't believe I lost so much, I forgive you Pa.

You closed your eyes, you died. I came through.

My opinions are still your views.

Optimistic pumping slut,

Oh yeah, rent is due.

Stop screaming I dont live with you.

The world I love, the ocean I love, broken windows can't stop.

She's so stuck; I love it, genders of a generation.

This world, I cannot stop.

Strum, higher, lower, yes.

You're beautiful, fast and great.

In my imaginary park,

Gregory M George

Porcelain,

I am your doll,

Break me.

He Senses Trouble

My father had no idea,

about the smoking in bathrooms, we never hurt the feces,

but the children,

all the children.

They will remember their place.

He had no idea.

about the cell.

Gregory M George

The Boys Believe

How many people have been pushed up, can I kiss your bra?

How many lonely views have you had?

Your lips don't touch my cigarette.

She has the bird's eyes, the powers.

Let's fight, step outside, the universe is bruised.

My injuries never want to end. They want to share this lonely life.

My shoes are old and this beer is way too sharp.

 Is it a broken mirror?

Mom, am I your best friend? Your bottom dropped out.

All the time,

aint no me, aint no you, aint no use.

Mood Puke

We are what they call stains.

Repeat, don't ever stop.

I love, bubble Gum, and psycho hairdressers.

Gregory M George

Superheroes Make Me Sick!

She stood to call me son, then she sang.
Be insane. That's ok, if it's in your soul.
I'm not a coward, the sun told me so.

It's oh, so very wet, she told me while waiting.
this is your second chance.
I know you don't feel good enough, it's hard.
I stood in front of your bird, and watched it die.

Is this ok?

Released, it sang.
So did I, it sung.
So did I, it flew.
I stayed. It was too quick of an end.

Mothers Against Everything

Random flowers grow in
random places for a reason.

Gregory M George

Uncontrollable Shaking

The poets are here, there's nothing wrong.
Are you supposed to be here?
Strong.

You showed me the rivers, the piano stayed.
Are you ready? Because I'm scared,
little boy why are you destroying that suitcase?
I promise that old women's lungs are not mad.

Hate

I'm not very sure how it feels to live every day.
I was so over obsessed, and missed the clumsy dog.
I looked around this city I was so tired of.
These pills never let me die for my sins,
this private world, broke my television.

We will never make a difference.
Will there be black clouds on the moon?
There's nothing left to take my place,
I am here.
Don't ever tell me I'm not that strong.

I am a very horny angel,

for that, I am sorry.

Gregory M George

They Hang At Night

Mr Writer, why don't you tell it like it is?
Take off that fucking makeup.
I'd rather pray to those who made you.
I have compassion, for when I bleed.
Through my waste, I cursed the holes in my body.

I'm so lonely,
you don't even know.

Movie Star Paradise

I know you're wondering when someone is going to follow you home.

Oh, I know you.

You're always looking for somebody to please, but no it's not me,

Oh no.

It's not me that you're looking for,
you just need a friend, to watch over you.

Gregory M George

Dressed to Kill

Who cleaned the kitchen from all the stains,
smoke rises so true into the roof, Mary I love you too.
girl you clean me, through my veins..
oh I love you Mary Jane,

the windows cleans from the cold nights shame,
Im so clean, I cannot refuse my beautiful cocaine,
through my veins, im happy with you.
oh let me tast the surprise, I fish into the wild,
I fish, I fish, im covered in bleach and anti biotics,
Is it bad I just cannot stop myself from wanting it,

I thought to myself,

Oh there she is, there she is.
I love you, I love you, I love you, Hate. Hate. I dream of you.

Let Her Three

Do you know what, its like to be clever?
The moment you're noticed, you're nothing at all.

Gregory M George

Black

I asked the spiders to remove my piano, and there was my plan.
I found another you.
Take your time,

still covered in confidence that I was once a coward.

Upper your voice, like throwing a mirror to my makeshift beauty,
I'm so hurt behind my words, I wish I could taste your sweat,
as my nose drips.

Confessions of the recruited innocent.
I was not willing.

Red Tattoo

He is a better man then I. I can feel this, so please don't ask.

You got such a beautiful mind; I wish I deserved it,

what you need in a man, I wish I could give.

That dandelion in your palm, the weed burns your hand,

there's a hole.

Are you sure you want a fertilized, un protected soul?

It's not a good soul.

A child can learn to use his teeth,

like the roots of a tree, and the life underneath.

Do you hate yourself, or are you too shy?

It's still young; it's supposed to be allowed to die.

I dont want to be in the water, it's not safe.

Liquid it's a mothers suicidal grave,

Don't say denial.

Fake

I was always the child in school who never wanted to mention the word addiction, the journalists, and the kid on prescription, addicted to the world of science fiction.

My humor was built on the fault line.
They would beg for my roots, to pull them out and strip them like trees, to gut my intestines of all the un-developed food and feces.

But when I broke the rules, the population grew,

It was a fanatic.

The Last Call

Speaking in tongues, the language of a drunk,

I get jealous of others creativity.

Color Blind

You never knew I was waiting for you.
The sounds were nothing but the truth.
Everybody knows.
How long is forever when you're a little kid?
She wore only black, but she was buried alone.

She screamed,
Shelter let me hide! She died, mouth to mouth.
I never felt for her, because she loved me.

Cold Floors and Hot Ceilings

My hand hurts, and that's my mistake, I asked your mothers sincerity and company.

Sincere she cannot plead,

worries and placements are factors against me. I politely asked for your hand in stake, A little bird told me that your type is too ripe to take.

I politely nod and take my due, if I ever leave don't think I would forget you.

My debt is so far into myself, I'm so uptight.

Repeats

Felt your ceramic smoke on my truth, and truthfully,

I never enjoyed drinking straight tea,

All of it,

...I lived in a piss stained mattress for years,

can you believe, were healthy.

Shave Me Fifth Third

My knees are too cold to touch,
my soul is too naive to budge.
I wouldn't care if they just disappeared.

And if you want to help,
don't be afraid to ask someone else.
I don't shit on your pity,
so don't shave me dry.

Run me down, and follow me home.
Everybody's lost something,
and im alone, and paranoid.

Shave me.

Hero

You crushed me from far above,

We fell like angels with sloppy love.

Top floor you are bound to crush me, I can't be hurt anymore.
I broke all the artifacts you and mom called things.
I broke my guitar in half, and ripped out the piano strings.
Music is magic, and my savior cannot save you now.
That must leave you weaponless what are you left to use,

that our game can allow?
Love cannot be an option, it's over used and defeated in my life.

I watched her walk away, into the time of when we never met.
I looked into the ocean, and it gave a proposal I couldn't regret,
She gave me the glass, and it would only be for my use.
She gave me the opportunity I couldn't refuse.

I just want you to be there when I'm home,
I need you to see me when I cannot.
I cannot do it alone,
I need you to be home.
She said with this advantage in life, you cannot lie.
You are banished from respect, and not allowed to see the sky.
You may keep your talent of the art forms, but nothing to show your smile. I promised, I promised that.

All The Children Died

Marcy bought the flowers,
Marcy bought me my gun,
Marcy bought the whole damn playschool something fun.

Marcy was a simple man,
Marcy had his only way,
I never had the proposal of ever getting into his ways,
he was a single man, he was insane.

Shoot, shoot.

Gregory M George

<u>Cat Scratch</u>

Sundays were always my worst days.

Dirty Love For You

I am drunk with the heavens
I keep stealing drinks from the streets,
the angels scream,
while the devil persists on having sex with me,

I do not believe, I believe in love,
I believe, I do not believe in love.

Save me from something that gets me all used,
I am alive, I'm feeling used, I'm starting too,

I'm starting to love you, I love you.
everything I need is in your veins,
through your spinal love, im coming to your brain.
I'm your drug, and im all about you,
I'm your next substance,
make me abused.

Gregory M George

I'm Always A Work In Progress

I never had a father,
razor burn.
A face with no shave,

Back roads called me names,
so did my imaginary friends.

When the teacher put the ruler down against my hands.

Audience of None

I'm so old now, everything is losing its addiction,
I smoke my last cigarette as the world falls apart.
I made a promise, sexual handshakes from the start,

Walk away, I know, I will always be after you,
what you say, is known to me as literary review,
I hide, forget me, follow through.

The other side is colorful, I'm color blind,
I use to be your biggest fan, you told me,
when your older you will understand,
and you hurt me, you killed me.
your only fan.

Gregory M George

She drinks soup

Ill promise to see through the bleach,

Ill tie my tongue in knots

Ill never lie again,

If you let me be your man.

<u>Cinema</u>

I use to walk
her home
she
was never one
to talk
no bubblegum
stuck between

her teeth

She sang about
that
time we
would meet the reptiles

Those walks
were
never wasted,

I listened
to music
in

her basement.

I Want To Ride My Bike

They sounded like slaves,

tortured but pleased

they would cry

Rubbing themselves

with dis respect and

recycled morals

I laughed

snorted

and ate

before I went to sleep.

Mailbox

The boy picked up

the lubricated telephone

Between his fingers

he held the news

Mother he cried;

the phones for you.

The smell

of lavender

she approached the boy

What a disgusting

smile your father has given you.

Gregory M George

Firefly

I was on the corner,
waiting for the lights to come on,
that's when I knew I was alone.

The city grew tired of me walking around,
the flame in my character
had burnt out.

<u>Last Call</u>

I don't want to be famous or inherit any of the popularity,

I just want to be heard.

If you made it this far, I'm assuming you read the entire collection of poetry or you just briefly skimmed through it and found yourself at a page that makes just a little bit of sense in comparison to what you have previously been viewing.

I couldn't put everything I have written into this book, but I chose very wisely what I wanted involved and what I wanted left out.
There was a lot left out but I'm sure they will make a few appearances in the future.

I really hope you enjoyed the poetry and art that comes with writing, the way the words can move your mind.

Peace and Love,

Love,

Love,

Mitchell George.

ABOUT THE AUTHOUR

Mitchell George was Born and Raised in Calgary AB; he is still a student and continues to grow artistically, emotionally, and physically. He plans to become a writer one day while expanding his knowledge by working with people who have been through the same lifestyle that he has.

He currently resides in Airdrie AB, with his loving brothers, and his cat Motorboat.

Don't forget to stay tuned for Becoming the Buffalo & other titles available by: Gregory M George.

Shelter The Messenger

Made in the USA
Charleston, SC
05 December 2011